Contents

Cheesy Mexican Soup
(p. 12)

Smokey Chipotle Salad
(p. 20)

Pasta Fagioli
(p. 18)

Near East Steak Salad
(p. 10)

Soups & Salads

Chicken Tortellini Soup

6 cups chicken broth
1 package (9 ounces) refrigerated cheese and spinach tortellini or three-cheese tortellini
1 package (about 6 ounces) refrigerated fully cooked chicken breast strips, cut into bite-size pieces
2 cups coarsely chopped baby spinach leaves
4 to 6 tablespoons grated Parmesan cheese
1 tablespoon chopped chives or 2 tablespoons sliced green onions

1. Bring chicken broth to a boil in large saucepan over high heat. Add tortellini. Reduce heat to medium; cook 5 minutes. Stir in chicken and spinach.

2. Reduce heat to low; cook 3 minutes or until chicken is heated through. Sprinkle with Parmesan cheese and chives.

Makes 4 servings

Spicy Chicken Apple Salad

Prep Time: 15 minutes

¼ cup HELLMANN'S® or BEST FOODS® Canola Real Mayonnaise
¼ cup jalapeño pepper jelly or mango chutney
8 cups mixed salad greens or baby spinach leaves
2 cups cut-up cooked chicken
1 medium Red or Golden Delicious apple, thinly sliced

1. In small bowl, combine Hellmann's or Best Foods Canola Real Mayonnaise with jelly; set aside.

2. To serve, arrange salad greens on serving platter, then top with chicken, apple and reserved mayonnaise mixture.

Makes 4 servings

Tip: Also terrific with Hellmann's® or Best Foods® Light Mayonnaise.

Roasted Red Pepper, Corn & Garbanzo Bean Salad

2 cans (15 ounces each) garbanzo beans
1 jar (16 ounces) GUILTLESS GOURMET® Roasted Red Pepper Salsa
1 cup frozen whole kernel corn, thawed and drained
2 green onions, thinly sliced
8 lettuce leaves
   Fresh tomato wedges and sunflower sprouts (optional)

Rinse and drain beans well; place in 2-quart casserole dish. Add roasted red pepper salsa, corn and onions; stir to combine. Cover and refrigerate 1 hour or up to 24 hours.

To serve, line serving platter with lettuce. Spoon bean mixture over top. Garnish with tomatoes and sprouts, if desired.

Makes 8 servings

Ham & Potato Soup

Prep Time: 5 minutes • **Cook Time:** 25 minutes

1 package (5 ounces) scalloped potatoes plus ingredients as package directs
1 bag (16 ounces) BIRDS EYE® frozen Broccoli Cuts
½ pound cooked ham, cut into ½-inch cubes
½ cup shredded Cheddar cheese (optional)

• Prepare potatoes according to package directions for stove top method, adding broccoli and ham when adding milk and butter.

• Stir in cheese just before serving.

Makes 4 servings

Serving Suggestion: Spoon mixture into shallow casserole dish. Sprinkle with cheese; broil until lightly browned.

Salmon Salad Monterey with Lemon-Dijon Vinaigrette

Prep Time: 20 minutes • **Broiling Time:** 9 minutes

3 tablespoons olive or vegetable oil
1½ tablespoons lemon juice
1½ teaspoons chopped chives
1 teaspoon honey
½ teaspoon Dijon mustard
1¼ pounds salmon fillet, skin removed
1 package (8 to 12 ounces) DOLE® Hearts of Romaine Salad Blend (or any variety)
1 cup red seedless grapes, halved
¼ to ⅓ cup chopped walnuts, toasted
Fresh chives, grape clusters and lemon slices (optional)

• Combine oil, lemon juice, chives, honey and mustard in jar. Cover; shake well.

• Preheat broiler. Cut fillet into 4 pieces; place on lightly oiled broiler pan. Brush salmon with some of the salad dressing. Broil salmon 4 inches from heat for 7 to 9 minutes or until fish flakes easily with fork.

• Toss together salad blend, grapes and walnuts. Spoon salad mixture onto four plates. Place one piece of salmon over each salad. Shake dressing; drizzle over each salad. Garnish with fresh chives, grape clusters and lemon slices, if desired. *Makes 4 servings*

Near East Steak Salad

Prep Time: 10 minutes • **Cook Time:** 10 minutes

⅔ cup *French's*® Honey Dijon Mustard
½ cup water
¼ cup teriyaki sauce
2 tablespoons grated peeled ginger
1 teaspoon minced garlic
1 pound boneless sirloin (1 inch thick) or flank steak
8 cups mixed salad greens, washed and torn
1 medium yellow or orange bell pepper, thinly sliced
2 green onions, thinly shredded
¼ cup chopped dry roasted peanuts

1. Combine mustard, water, teriyaki sauce, ginger and garlic in small bowl. Pour 1 cup dressing into small serving bowl.

2. Broil or grill steak 10 minutes or until desired doneness, basting with remaining ½ cup dressing. Let stand 5 minutes.

3. Thinly slice steak. Serve over salad greens. Top with bell pepper, green onions and peanuts. Drizzle with reserved dressing.

Makes 4 servings

*Tip

For speedy yet fresh meals, use timesaving convenience products such as presliced pepper strips or carrots from the produce department of your supermarket. The salad bar is another place to find cut up vegetables that help you get a home-cooked meal on the table more quickly.

Cheesy Mexican Soup

1 cup chopped onion
1 tablespoon vegetable oil
2 cups milk
1 can (about 14 ounces) chicken broth
1 container (13 ounces) ORTEGA® Salsa & Cheese Bowl
1 can (7 ounces) ORTEGA Diced Green Chiles
4 ORTEGA Taco Shells, crushed
¼ cup chopped cilantro

COOK and stir onion in oil in large saucepan over medium-high heat for 4 to 6 minutes until tender. Reduce heat to medium-low.

STIR in milk, chicken broth, Salsa & Cheese and green chiles; cook for 5 to 7 minutes until hot, stirring frequently.

MICROWAVE crushed taco shells on HIGH (100%) 30 to 45 seconds. Cool. Serve soup sprinkled with cilantro and crushed taco shells. *Makes 8 servings*

Note: If you can't find a 7-ounce can of ORTEGA® Diced Green Chiles, use two 4-ounce cans.

*Tip

Crush taco shells quickly and easily by placing them in a sealed food storage bag, then running a rolling pin over the bag several times to pulverize them.

Grilled Steak with Arugula & Gorgonzola Salad

4 beef top loin (strip) steaks (¾ inch thick)
1 cup balsamic or red wine salad dressing, divided
2 cups baby arugula leaves
2 cups mixed salad greens
½ cup crumbled Gorgonzola cheese

1. Place steaks in large resealable food storage bag; pour ½ cup salad dressing into bag. Seal bag; turn to coat. Marinate in refrigerator 20 to 30 minutes. Meanwhile, prepare grill for direct cooking.

2. Remove steaks from marinade; discard marinade. Place steaks on grid over medium-high heat. Grill, covered, 6 to 8 minutes for medium-rare (145°F) or until desired doneness, turning once.

3. Meanwhile, combine arugula and salad greens. Pour remaining ½ cup dressing over greens; toss until greens are well coated. Serve steaks with salad. Sprinkle with cheese.   *Makes 4 servings*

*Tip

If you can't find Gorgonzola, substitute your favorite blue cheese.

Chopped Salad Tostadas

1 package (10) ORTEGA® Tostada Shells
6 cups shredded iceberg lettuce
1 cup shredded carrot
1 can (2.25 ounces) sliced ripe olives, coarsely chopped
1 tomato, seeded, chopped and drained
⅓ cup ranch dressing
6 tablespoons ORTEGA Taco Sauce (any variety), divided
1 can (16 ounces) ORTEGA Refried Beans
10 tablespoons shredded Mexican blend cheese

HEAT tostada shells according to package directions. Meanwhile, in large bowl, gently toss lettuce, carrot, olives and tomato.

MIX ranch dressing and 2 tablespoons taco sauce in small bowl. Pour dressing over lettuce mixture; toss gently to coat.

COMBINE refried beans and remaining 4 tablespoons taco sauce in saucepan; heat over medium heat until warm.

SPREAD each tostada shell with 3 tablespoons bean mixture; top with about ¾ cup salad mixture and sprinkle with cheese.

Makes 10 tostadas

Note: Mexican blend cheese is a blend of four types of cheese. You can also use Cheddar or Monterey Jack cheese.

Pasta Fagioli

Prep Time: 20 minutes • **Cook Time:** 10 minutes

1 jar (1 pound 10 ounces) RAGÚ® Chunky Gardenstyle Pasta Sauce
1 can (19 ounces) white kidney beans, rinsed and drained
1 box (10 ounces) frozen chopped spinach, thawed
8 ounces ditalini pasta, cooked and drained (reserve 2 cups pasta water)

1. In 6-quart saucepot, combine Ragú Pasta Sauce, beans, spinach, pasta and reserved pasta water; heat through.

2. Season, if desired, with salt, ground black pepper and grated Parmesan cheese.   *Makes 4 servings*

Chicken Caesar Salad

Prep and Cook Time: 20 minutes

6 ounces chicken tenders
¼ cup plus 1 tablespoon Caesar salad dressing, divided
Black pepper
4 cups (about 5 ounces) prepared Italian salad mix
½ cup croutons, divided
2 tablespoons grated Parmesan cheese

1. Cut chicken tenders in half lengthwise and crosswise. Heat 1 tablespoon salad dressing in large nonstick skillet. Add chicken; cook and stir over medium heat 3 to 4 minutes or until chicken is cooked through. Remove from skillet. Season with pepper; let cool.

2. Combine salad mix, ¼ cup croutons, remaining ¼ cup salad dressing and Parmesan cheese in serving bowl; toss to coat. Top with chicken and remaining ¼ cup croutons.   *Makes 2 servings*

Smokey Chipotle Salad

1 package (15.2 ounces) ORTEGA® Soft Taco Kit
2 tablespoons vegetable oil
¼ cup sour cream
3 tablespoons mayonnaise
2 small chipotle chiles in adobo sauce, seeded and finely chopped
1 pound ground beef
1 bag (15 ounces) romaine salad mix
1 cup (4 ounces) shredded Cheddar & Monterey Jack cheese
1 can (2.5 ounces) sliced ripe olives, drained

HEAT oven to 400°F. Brush each tortilla from Soft Taco Kit with ¼ teaspoon oil; cut into fourths. Place tortillas on 2 baking sheets. Bake 5 to 7 minutes or until lightly browned.

PREPARE dressing by combining sour cream, mayonnaise, chipotle chiles and taco sauce from kit; stir until blended.

COOK ground beef as directed on Soft Taco Kit using seasoning mix from kit.

TOSS romaine mix with chipotle dressing in large bowl until lightly coated.

ASSEMBLE each salad onto serving plates by layering 1½ cups romaine mixture, ⅔ cup beef mixture, 3 tablespoons cheese and 1½ tablespoons olives.

SERVE each salad with tortilla pieces.   *Makes 4 to 5 servings*

Note: Chipotle chiles in adobo sauce are dried, smoked jalapeños in seasoned tomato sauce. They are available in 7- and 11-ounce cans.

Tuna Salad Stuffed Sweet Red Peppers

2 cans (6 ounces each) albacore tuna packed in water, drained
2 large stalks celery, diagonally sliced
½ cup halved green grapes
½ cup (2 ounces) shredded sharp Cheddar cheese
⅓ cup mayonnaise
   Salt and black pepper
2 red bell peppers, seeded and halved

1. Combine tuna, celery, grapes, cheese and mayonnaise in medium bowl; blend well. Season with salt and black pepper.

2. Divide tuna mixture evenly between hollowed bell pepper halves.   *Makes 4 servings*

Mandarin Chicken Salad

1 package (5 to 12 ounces) DOLE® American or Italian Salad Blend or other variety
3 boneless, skinless chicken breasts, cooked, shredded or chopped (9 ounces)
1 can (11 or 15 ounces) DOLE® Mandarin Oranges, drained
½ cup pea pods or bean sprouts (optional)
¼ cup chopped DOLE® Green Onions
½ cup oriental or oriental chicken salad dressing
½ cup chow mein noodles or fried wonton strips

• Combine salad blend, chicken, mandarin oranges, pea pods and green onions in large bowl.

• Pour dressing over salad; toss to evenly coat. Sprinkle noodles over salad; serve.   *Makes 4 servings*

Taco Topped Baked Potato
(p. 30)

Easy Barbecue Sloppy Joe
(p. 34)

Layered Mexican Casserole
(p. 32)

Family-Style Beef Pizza
(p. 28)

Ground Meat Mains

String Cheese Spaghetti & Meatballs

Prep Time: 20 minutes • **Cook Time:** 20 minutes

1 pound ground beef
½ cup Italian seasoned dry bread crumbs
1 egg
1 jar (1 pound 10 ounces) RAGÚ® Organic Pasta Sauce
1 cup cubed mozzarella cheese (about 4 ounces)
8 ounces regular or whole wheat spaghetti, cooked
and drained

1. In medium bowl, combine ground beef, bread crumbs and egg; shape into 12 meatballs.

2. In 3-quart saucepan, bring Pasta Sauce to a boil over medium-high heat. Gently stir in uncooked meatballs.

3. Reduce heat to low and simmer covered, stirring occasionally, 20 minutes or until meatballs are done. To serve, toss meatballs and sauce with mozzarella cheese and hot spaghetti.

Makes 4 servings

*Tip

Italian bread crumbs contain added parsley flakes, garlic powder and occasionally other seasonings and Parmesan cheese. They boost flavor without needing to add more seasoning.

Family-Style Beef Pizza

Prep Time: 20 minutes • **Bake Time:** 12 to 18 minutes

- 1 package (about 14 ounces) refrigerated pizza dough
- ¼ pound ground beef
- 3 tablespoons finely chopped onion
- ¾ cup pizza sauce
- 1 small tomato, peeled, seeded and chopped
- 2 teaspoons Italian seasoning
- 2 cloves garlic, minced
- ⅛ teaspoon ground red pepper
- ½ cup sliced mushrooms
- 1 cup (4 ounces) shredded part-skim mozzarella cheese
- 1 tablespoon finely grated Parmesan cheese

1. Preheat oven to 425°F. Lightly spray 12-inch pizza pan with nonstick cooking spray. Unroll pizza dough; press onto prepared pan. Build up edges slightly. Prick dough all over with fork. Bake 7 to 10 minutes or until lightly browned.

2. Meanwhile, brown ground beef with onion in large skillet, stirring to break up meat; drain.

3. Combine pizza sauce, tomato, Italian seasoning, garlic and red pepper in small saucepan over medium heat; bring to a boil. Reduce heat; simmer, uncovered, about 8 minutes or until thickened.

4. Spread tomato mixture evenly over pizza crust. Sprinkle with ground beef mixture, mushrooms then cheeses. Return to oven. Bake 5 to 8 minutes more or until heated through.

Makes 6 servings

Taco Topped Baked Potatoes

4 large baking potatoes, scrubbed
½ pound (8 ounces) ground beef
¼ cup chopped onion
1 package (1.25 ounces) ORTEGA® Taco Seasoning Mix
1 container (13 ounces) ORTEGA Salsa & Cheese Bowl
  Salt to taste
  Sour cream (optional)

PRICK potatoes several times with a fork. Microwave on HIGH (100%) uncovered, 12 to 15 minutes or until just tender, turning potatoes over and re-arranging once.

CRUMBLE ground beef into 1 quart glass casserole; add onion. Microwave on HIGH (100%) uncovered, 3 to 3½ minutes or until meat is set, stirring once; drain.

STIR in taco seasoning and half the amount of water specified on taco seasoning package. Add contents of Salsa & Cheese Bowl. Cover; microwave on HIGH (100%) 2½ to 3 minutes or until heated through, stirring once.

MAKE a crosswise slash in each potato; press side of potato to form an opening. Sprinkle with salt. Spoon filling into potatoes.

TOP each potato with sour cream, if desired.   *Makes 4 servings*

*Tip

Baking potatoes have a high starch and low moisture content. Long-shaped potatoes are the most suitable for baking. These potatoes will fluff up better when microwaved or baked.

Magically Moist Turkey Burgers

Prep Time: 10 minutes • **Cook Time:** 10 minutes

1¼ **pounds ground turkey**
½ **cup finely chopped orange or red bell pepper**
⅓ **cup HELLMANN'S® or BEST FOODS® Real Mayonnaise**
¼ **cup plain dry bread crumbs**
2 **tablespoons finely chopped sweet onion**
2 **tablespoons finely chopped fresh parsley (optional)**
½ **teaspoon salt (optional)**

In medium bowl, combine all ingredients; shape into 6 burgers. Grill or broil until done. Serve, if desired, on hamburger buns with your favorite toppings. *Makes 6 servings*

Skillet Sausage with Potatoes and Rosemary

1 **tablespoon vegetable oil**
3 **cups diced red skin potatoes**
1 **cup diced onion**
1 **pound BOB EVANS® Original Recipe Roll Sausage**
½ **teaspoon dried rosemary**
¼ **teaspoon rubbed sage**
   Salt and black pepper to taste
2 **tablespoons chopped fresh parsley**

Heat oil in large skillet over medium-high heat 1 minute. Add potatoes; cook 5 to 10 minutes or until slightly brown, stirring occasionally. Add onion; cook until tender. Add crumbled sausage; cook until browned. Add rosemary, sage, salt and pepper; cook and stir until well blended. Transfer to serving platter and garnish with parsley. Refrigerate leftovers. *Makes 4 to 6 servings*

Layered Mexican Casserole

- **½ pound ground beef**
- **1 (12-ounce) can whole kernel corn, drained**
- **1 (12-ounce) jar chunky salsa**
- **1 (2¼-ounce) can sliced pitted ripe olives, drained**
- **1 cup cream-style cottage cheese**
- **1 (8-ounce) carton dairy sour cream**
- **5 cups tortilla chips (7 to 8 ounces)**
- **2 cups (8 ounces) shredded Wisconsin Cheddar cheese, divided**
- **½ cup chopped tomato**

Brown ground beef in large skillet; drain. Add corn and salsa; cook until thoroughly heated. Reserve 2 tablespoons olives; stir remaining olives into beef mixture.

Combine cottage cheese and sour cream in bowl. In 2-quart casserole, layer 2 cups chips, half of meat mixture, ¾ cup Cheddar cheese and half of cottage cheese mixture. Repeat layers; cover.

Bake in preheated 350°F oven 35 minutes. Line edge of casserole with remaining 1 cup chips; top with tomato, reserved 2 tablespoons olives and remaining ½ cup Cheddar cheese. Bake 10 minutes or until cheese is melted and chips are hot.

Makes 4 to 6 servings

Favorite recipe from **Wisconsin Milk Marketing Board**

Easy Barbecue Sloppy Joes

Prep Time: 10 minutes • **Cook Time:** 15 minutes

1 pound lean ground beef or turkey
1 small onion, chopped
1 green bell pepper, chopped
1 can (10¾ ounces) condensed cream of tomato soup
    or tomato bisque, undiluted
¼ cup prepared barbecue sauce
½ teaspoon salt
½ teaspoon hot pepper sauce (optional)
4 BAYS® English Muffins, split, lightly toasted
4 slices American or Cheddar cheese, cut in half
    diagonally

Crumble meat into large deep skillet; add onion and bell pepper. Cook over medium heat until meat is no longer pink, stirring occasionally. Pour off drippings. Add soup, barbecue sauce, salt and hot pepper sauce; simmer uncovered 8 minutes, stirring occasionally. Serve over split muffins topped with cheese.

Makes 4 servings

*Tip

When buying ground beef, read the label to determine the percent of lean. You can find ground beef with 95%, 90%, 85% and 80% lean. When preparing Sloppy Joes, 90% or 95% lean are good choices since additional seasonings and sauces add flavor.

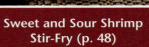

Sweet and Sour Shrimp
Stir-Fry (p. 48)

Spicy Caribbean Pork
Medallions (p. 40)

Tuna Monte Cristo Sandwich
(p. 46)

Chili Cranberry Chicken
(p. 38)

Effortless Entrées

Chili Cranberry Chicken

½ cup HEINZ® Chili Sauce
½ cup whole berry cranberry sauce
2 tablespoons orange marmalade
⅛ teaspoon ground allspice
4 to 6 skinless boneless chicken breast halves
(about 1½ pounds)
2 teaspoons vegetable oil

Combine first 4 ingredients; set aside. In large skillet, slowly brown chicken on both sides in oil. Pour reserved chili sauce mixture over chicken. Simmer, uncovered, 8 to 10 minutes or until chicken is cooked and sauce is of desired consistency, turning and basting occasionally.   *Makes 4 to 6 servings and about 1 cup sauce*

Cinnamon Apple Pork Chops

4 boneless pork chops
2 tablespoons vegetable oil
1 jar (12 ounces) HEINZ® HomeStyle Pork Gravy
½ cup raisins
1 tablespoon honey
1½ teaspoons cinnamon
Dash allspice
1 tart cooking apple, thinly sliced
Hot cooked rice

In large skillet, cook pork chops in oil until browned on both sides; season with salt and pepper. Stir in gravy, raisins, honey, cinnamon and allspice. Cover and simmer 15 minutes or until pork chops are tender. Add apple; cook 5 minutes longer or until apple slices are tender. Serve with hot rice.   *Makes 4 servings*

Spicy Caribbean Pork Medallions

6 ounces pork tenderloin
1 teaspoon Caribbean jerk seasoning
· **Olive oil cooking spray**
⅓ cup pineapple juice
1 teaspoon brown mustard
½ teaspoon cornstarch

1. Cut tenderloin into ½-inch-thick slices. Place each slice between 2 pieces of plastic wrap. Pound to ¼-inch thickness. Rub both sides of pork pieces with jerk seasoning.

2. Lightly spray large nonstick skillet with cooking spray; heat over medium heat until hot. Add pork. Cook 2 to 3 minutes or until no longer pink, turning once. Remove from skillet. Keep warm.

3. Stir together pineapple juice, mustard and cornstarch until smooth. Add to skillet. Cook and stir over medium heat until mixture comes to a boil and thickens slightly. Spoon over pork.

Makes 2 servings

*Tip

To make your own Caribbean Jerk Seasoning, combine salt, thyme, red pepper, and allspice in equal amounts, adding more or less seasoning to suit your taste. Store extra seasoning in a tightly covered jar in a cool, dry place.

Santa Fe Fish Fillets with Mango-Cilantro Salsa

Nonstick cooking spray
1½ **pounds fish fillets (cod, perch or tilapia, about
½ inch thick)**
½ **package (3 tablespoons) ORTEGA® Taco Seasoning
Mix**
3 **ORTEGA Taco Shells, finely crushed**
1 **cup ORTEGA Salsa, any variety**
½ **cup diced mango**
2 **tablespoons chopped cilantro**

PREHEAT oven to 375°F. Cover broiler pan with foil. Spray with cooking spray.

DIP fish fillets in taco seasoning mix, coating both sides; place on foil. Spray coated fillets with cooking spray. Sprinkle with crushed taco shells.

BAKE 15 to 20 minutes until flaky in center.

MICROWAVE salsa on HIGH (100%) 1 minute. Stir in mango and cilantro.

SPOON salsa over fish before serving.   *Makes 4 to 6 servings*

*Tip

If fresh mangoes are not available, look for refrigerated jars of sliced mango in the produce section of most supermarkets.

Broiled Lemon Chicken

4 skinless boneless chicken breast halves
¼ cup HEINZ® Worcestershire Sauce
2 tablespoons lemon juice
1 teaspoon minced garlic
½ teaspoon pepper
½ teaspoon grated lemon peel
Vegetable oil

Lightly flatten chicken breasts to uniform thickness. For marinade, combine Worcestershire sauce and next 4 ingredients; pour over chicken. Cover; marinate 30 minutes, turning once. Place chicken on broiler pan, brush with oil; broil 3 to 4 minutes on each side.

Makes 4 servings

Turkey Teriyaki

2 tablespoons low-sodium soy sauce
2 tablespoons cooking sherry or apple juice
1 tablespoon canola oil
1 teaspoon ground ginger
1 teaspoon packed light brown sugar
1 clove garlic, minced
½ teaspoon black pepper
1 pound turkey or chicken cutlets
Additional canola oil (optional)

Combine all ingredients except turkey in small bowl; mix well. Place turkey in resealable plastic food storage bag. Pour soy sauce mixture over turkey; seal bag. Refrigerate several hours.

Remove turkey from bag; discard marinade. Grill 18 to 25 minutes or sauté in 1 teaspoon canola oil in skillet over medium heat until meat is no longer pink in center. *Makes 4 servings*

*Favorite recipe from **CanolaInfo***

Peachy Smothered Pork Chops

Prep Time: 5 minutes • **Cook Time:** 25 minutes

**1 tablespoon vegetable oil
1 small onion, finely minced
1 (12-ounce) jar peach preserves
⅔ cup *French's®* Honey Mustard
2 teaspoons grated peeled gingerroot
¼ teaspoon ground nutmeg
6 boneless pork chops, cut 1-inch thick**

1. Heat oil in small saucepan; sauté onion until tender. Stir in peach preserves, mustard, ginger and nutmeg.

2. Grill or broil chops over medium direct heat 20 minutes until barely pink in center, turning and basting often with sauce.

3. Serve chops with reserved sauce mixture.   *Makes 6 servings*

Alternate Method: For alternate skillet method, brown chops in skillet. Pour peach mixture over chops and simmer until no longer pink in center.

Tuna Monte Cristo Sandwiches

Prep and Cook Time: 20 minutes

4 slices (½ ounce each) Cheddar cheese
4 oval slices sourdough or challah (egg) bread
½ pound deli tuna salad
¼ cup milk
1 egg, beaten
2 tablespoons butter

1. Place 1 slice cheese on each of 2 bread slices. Spread tuna salad evenly over two slices of cheese. Top each with remaining cheese and bread slices.

2. Combine milk and egg in shallow bowl; stir until well blended. Dip sandwiches in egg mixture, turning to coat well.

3. Melt butter in large nonstick skillet over medium heat. Add sandwiches; cook 4 to 5 minutes per side or until cheese melts and sandwiches are golden brown.   *Makes 2 servings*

*Tip

A Monte Cristo sandwich is dipped into beaten egg and grilled in butter until golden brown. The classic Monte Cristo sandwich consists of ham, turkey or chicken and Swiss cheese on buttered bread and is served with a side of raspberry or strawberry jam or cranberry sauce for dipping.

Tuna Monte Cristo Sandwich

Sweet and Sour
Shrimp Stir-Fry

   1 tablespoon dark sesame oil
   ½ cup thinly sliced celery
   ¼ cup chopped red bell pepper
   ¼ cup chopped green onions
   ½ teaspoon ground ginger
   1 teaspoon soy sauce
   1 teaspoon lemon juice
   1 teaspoon sugar
   1 pound medium raw shrimp, peeled and deveined

1. Heat oil in large nonstick skillet over medium heat. Add celery, bell pepper, green onions and ginger. Cook and stir 5 to 7 minutes.

2. Add soy sauce, lemon juice and sugar; cook and stir 1 minute. Add shrimp; cook 3 minutes or until shrimp are pink and opaque.

Makes 4 servings

Bayou Shrimp

   1 medium green pepper, cut into 1-inch chunks
   1 clove garlic, minced
   1 tablespoon vegetable oil
   1 can (14½ ounces) stewed tomatoes
   ½ cup HEINZ® Chili Sauce
   ¼ to ½ teaspoon hot pepper sauce
   1 pound medium-size raw shrimp, shelled and deveined
   Hot cooked rice (optional)

In large skillet, cook and stir green pepper and garlic in oil 1 minute. Stir in tomatoes, chili sauce and hot pepper sauce; simmer about 4 minutes or until slightly thickened, stirring occasionally. Stir in shrimp; simmer 3 to 4 minutes or until shrimp turn pink and opaque. Serve over rice. *Makes 4 servings*

Baked Potato Salad with Chipotle Ranch Dressing

Prep Time: 10 minutes

- 1 cup *French's® Gourmayo™* **Smoked Chipotle Light Mayonnaise**
- ½ cup **reduced-fat sour cream**
- 1 teaspoon **finely minced garlic**
- 4 **hot baked potatoes**
- 4 cups **shredded or chopped vegetables from salad bar (such as zucchini, carrots, broccoli, red bell peppers)**
- 1 cup *French's®* **Cheddar French Fried Onions**

1. Stir together mayonnaise, sour cream and garlic in serving bowl; set aside.

2. Split tops of potatoes lengthwise. Squeeze each potato from ends to open wide. Place on serving plates.

3. Spoon vegetables on top of potatoes, dividing evenly. Sprinkle with French Fried Onions and serve with dressing.

Makes 4 servings

*Tip

To save time, microwave potatoes 10 to 12 minutes on HIGH.

Curried Shrimp and Noodles
(p. 56)

Chipotle Chicken Quesadillas
(p. 66)

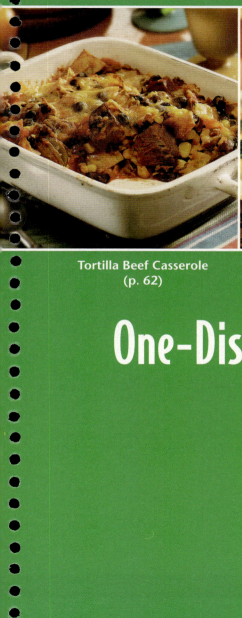

Tortilla Beef Casserole
(p. 62)

Penne with Roasted Chicken
& Vegetables (p. 60)

One-Dish Meals

Tortellini Bake Parmesano

Prep and Cook Time: 35 minutes

1 package (12 ounces) fresh or frozen cheese tortellini or ravioli
½ pound lean ground beef
½ medium onion, finely chopped
2 cloves garlic, minced
½ teaspoon dried oregano, crushed
1 can (26 ounces) DEL MONTE® Chunky Spaghetti Sauce with Garlic & Herb
2 small zucchini, sliced
⅓ cup (about 1½ ounces) grated Parmesan cheese

1. Cook pasta according to package directions; rinse and drain.

2. Meanwhile, brown beef with onion, garlic and oregano in large skillet over medium-high heat; drain. Season with salt and pepper, if desired.

3. Add spaghetti sauce and zucchini. Cook 15 minutes or until thickened, stirring occasionally.

4. Arrange half of pasta in oiled 2-quart microwavable dish; top with half each of sauce and cheese. Repeat layers ending with cheese; cover.

5. Microwave on HIGH 8 to 10 minutes or until heated through, rotating dish halfway through cooking time.   *Makes 4 servings*

Hint: For convenience, double recipe and freeze one half for later use. The recipe can also be made ahead, refrigerated and heated just before serving (allow extra time in microwave if dish is chilled).

Curried Shrimp and Noodles

3 cups water
2 packages (about 1.6 ounces each) instant
    curry-flavored rice noodle soup mix
1 package (8 ounces) frozen cooked baby shrimp
1 cup frozen bell pepper strips, cut into 1-inch pieces
    or 1 cup frozen peas
¼ cup chopped green onions
¼ teaspoon salt
¼ teaspoon black pepper
1 to 2 tablespoons fresh lime juice

1. Bring 3 cups water to a boil in large saucepan over high heat. Add soup mix, shrimp, bell pepper, green onions, salt and black pepper.

2. Cook 3 to 5 minutes, stirring frequently, or until noodles are tender. Stir in lime juice. Serve immediately.   *Makes 4 servings*

Vegetarian Jambalaya

1 tablespoon vegetable oil
½ cup diced green or red bell pepper
1 can (about 14 ounces) diced tomatoes with chiles
1 package (12 ounces) ground taco/burrito flavor
    soy meat substitute, crumbled
1 package (about 9 ounces) New Orleans style
    ready-to-serve jambalaya rice
2 tablespoons water

1. Heat oil in large skillet over medium-high heat. Add bell pepper; cook 3 minutes.

2. Add tomatoes, soy crumbles and rice; mix well. Stir in water. Cook 5 minutes, uncovered, or until heated through.
Makes 4 servings

Chili-Chicken Enchiladas

Nonstick cooking spray
3 cups (12 ounces) shredded Cheddar and/or
    Monterey Jack cheese, divided
1½ cups sour cream, divided
¾ cup roasted red peppers, drained, chopped and
    divided
1 can (7 ounces) ORTEGA® Diced Green Chiles, divided
2 cups diced cooked chicken
1 can (10 ounces) ORTEGA Enchilada Sauce
8 (8-inch) ORTEGA Soft Flour Tortillas

PREHEAT oven to 350°F. Spray 13×9-inch glass baking dish with cooking spray.

RESERVE 1½ cups cheese, ½ cup sour cream and ¼ cup each red peppers and green chiles; set aside.

MIX chicken with remaining cheese, sour cream, red peppers and green chiles in medium bowl.

SPREAD about 2 teaspoons enchilada sauce over each tortilla. Top each with about ½ cup chicken mixture. Roll up tortillas; arrange, seam side down, in baking dish.

TOP tortillas with remaining enchilada sauce. Sprinkle with the reserved cheese.

COVER with foil. Bake for 50 to 60 minutes or until hot, removing foil during last 5 minutes of baking time.

SPOON reserved sour cream over top and sprinkle with the reserved red peppers and green chiles.

Makes 4 servings (2 enchiladas each)

*Tip

Rotisserie chicken is a great time-saver for busy cooks. Try using it for the diced cooked chicken in this recipe.

Penne with Roasted Chicken & Vegetables

1 whole roasted chicken (about 2 pounds)
1 box (16 ounces) penne pasta
1 pound roasted vegetables, cut into bite-size pieces
⅓ cup shredded Parmesan cheese
Freshly ground black pepper

1. Remove chicken meat from bones and shred. Discard bones and skin.

2. Cook pasta according to package directions; drain and return to pan. Add chicken and vegetables; toss until heated through. Sprinkle with cheese and season with pepper. *Makes 6 servings*

*Tip

Cook twice as much pasta as you need one night and get a head start on the next pasta meal. Thoroughly drain the pasta you are not using immediately. Plunge it into a bowl of ice water to stop the cooking. Drain completely and toss with 1 or 2 tablespoons of olive oil. Cover and refrigerate up to 3 days. To reheat the pasta, microwave on HIGH 2 to 4 minutes, stirring halfway through.

Tortilla Beef Casserole

1 package (about 17 ounces) refrigerated fully cooked beef pot roast in gravy
6 (6-inch) corn tortillas, cut into 1-inch pieces
1 jar (16 ounces) salsa
1½ cups corn kernels
1 cup canned black or pinto beans, rinsed and drained
1 cup (4 ounces) shredded Mexican cheese blend

1. Preheat oven to 350°F. Lightly spray 11×7-inch or 2-quart casserole with nonstick cooking spray. Drain and discard gravy from pot roast; cut or shred beef into bite-size pieces.

2. Combine beef, tortillas, salsa, corn and beans in large bowl; mix well. Transfer to prepared casserole. Bake 20 minutes or until heated through. Sprinkle with cheese; bake 5 minutes more or until cheese is melted. *Makes 4 servings*

Creamy Chicken & Broccoli Alfredo

6 ounces uncooked fettuccini pasta
1½ cups fresh or frozen broccoli florets
1 small onion, sliced; slices cut in half
2 tablespoons butter or margarine
1 (10-ounce) can HORMEL® chunk breast of chicken, drained and flaked
1 (10-ounce) container refrigerated alfredo sauce

Cook pasta according to package directions. In large skillet, sauté broccoli and onion in butter until broccoli is crisp tender. Stir in chunk chicken and alfredo sauce. Cook, stirring constantly, until sauce is thoroughly heated. Serve over hot cooked pasta.
Makes 6 servings

Tortilla Beef Casserole

Chicken & Mushrooms with Pasta & Roasted Garlic Sauce

1 tablespoon olive oil
4 boneless skinless chicken breasts
1 jar (about 28 ounces) roasted garlic pasta sauce
1 cup sliced mushrooms
8 ounces rotini or fusilli pasta, cooked and drained
Grated Parmesan cheese (optional)

1. Heat oil in large skillet over medium heat. Lightly brown chicken. Remove from skillet; cut into thin strips. Return to skillet.

2. Stir in pasta sauce and mushrooms. Cover; simmer 10 minutes or until chicken is cooked through. Stir in pasta. Sprinkle with cheese, if desired. *Makes 4 servings*

Crunchy Veg•All® Tuna Casserole

2 cups cooked medium egg noodles
1 can (15 ounces) VEG•ALL® Original Mixed Vegetables, drained
1 can (12 ounces) solid white tuna in water, drained
1 can (10 ¾ ounces) cream of celery soup, undiluted
1¼ cups whole milk
½ cup sour cream
1 tablespoon chopped fresh dill
1 cup crushed sour cream & onion potato chips

Combine all ingredients except potato chips in greased 1½-quart casserole dish.

Microwave, uncovered, on High for 10 to 12 minutes or until very thick. Let cool for 10 minutes.

Top with crushed potato chips and serve. *Makes 4 to 6 servings*

Chipotle Chicken Quesadillas

1 package (8 ounces) cream cheese, softened
1 cup (4 ounces) shredded Mexican Cheddar Jack cheese
1 tablespoon minced chipotle pepper in adobo sauce
5 (10-inch) burrito-size flour tortillas
5 cups shredded cooked chicken (about 1¼ pounds)
   Nonstick cooking spray
   Guacamole, sour cream, salsa and fresh chopped cilantro

1. Combine cheeses and chipotle pepper in large bowl.

2. Spread ⅓ cup cheese mixture over half of tortilla. Top with about 1 cup chicken. Fold over tortilla. Repeat with remaining tortillas.

3. Heat large nonstick skillet over medium-high heat. Spray outside surface of each tortilla with nonstick cooking spray. Cook each tortilla 4 to 6 minutes or until lightly browned, turning once during cooking.

4. Cut each tortilla into 4 wedges. Serve with guacamole, sour cream, salsa and cilantro.   *Makes 5 servings (4 wedges each)*

*Tip

Chipotle peppers in adobo sauce can be found in cans in the Mexican food section of your grocery store.

Spinach Noodle Bowl with Ginger

6¼ cups chicken broth
4 ounces uncooked dry vermicelli noodles, broken into thirds
1½ cups matchstick carrots
3 ounces snow peas, cut in half, stems removed
4 cups packed spinach leaves (4 ounces)
1½ cups cooked diced chicken or shrimp
½ cup finely chopped green onions
1 tablespoon grated fresh ginger
1 teaspoon soy sauce
⅛ to ¼ teaspoon dried red pepper flakes

1. Bring broth to a boil in Dutch oven over high heat. Add vermicelli. Return to a boil; cook until al dente, about 2 minutes less than package instructions. Add carrots and snow peas; cook 2 minutes or until pasta is tender.

2. Remove from heat; add spinach, chicken, green onions, ginger, soy sauce and pepper flakes. Let stand 2 minutes to absorb flavors.

Makes 4 (1½ cup) servings

Note: Look for cooked, diced chicken in the refrigerated food section of your supermarket.

Chicken with Rice & Asparagus Pilaf

4 boneless skinless chicken breasts
3 teaspoons Poultry Seasoning, divided (recipe follows)
2 tablespoons olive oil
1 medium onion, chopped
1 cup uncooked rice
1 clove garlic, minced
2 cups chicken broth
¾ teaspoon salt
1 pound asparagus, trimmed and cut into 2-inch pieces (about 3 cups)

1. Sprinkle each chicken breast with ¼ teaspoon Poultry Seasoning. Heat oil in large skillet over medium-high heat. Brown chicken about 2 minutes on each side. Remove from skillet.

2. Add onion; cook and stir 3 minutes. Add rice and garlic; cook and stir 1 to 2 minutes. Add broth, remaining 2 teaspoons Poultry Seasoning and salt. Bring to a boil over high heat. Reduce heat to low; cook, covered, 5 minutes.

3. Stir in asparagus and chicken. Cook, covered, 10 to 12 minutes or until rice is tender and chicken is cooked through (165°F).

Makes 4 servings

Poultry Seasoning

¼ cup dried rosemary
¼ cup dried thyme
¼ cup dried marjoram
¼ cup rubbed sage
2 teaspoons black pepper

Combine all ingredients in small bowl; mix well. Pour herb mixture into ½-pint food storage jar with tight-fitting lid. Seal jar; store in cool place. Makes one ½-pint jar.

Fiesta-Style Roasted Vegetables
(p. 82)

Stovetop Summer Squash
(p. 78)

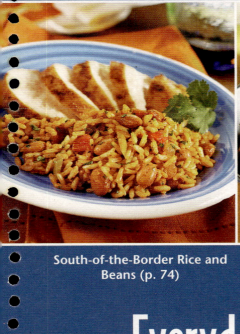

South-of-the-Border Rice and Beans (p. 74)

Spicy Skillet Vegetables, Salsa-Style (p. 80)

Everyday Sides

South-of-the-Border Rice and Beans

1¼ cups water
1 cup ORTEGA® Salsa, any variety
½ package (3 tablespoons) ORTEGA Taco Seasoning Mix
2 teaspoons vegetable oil
2 cups uncooked instant white rice
1 can (about 15 ounces) pinto beans, rinsed and drained
¼ cup chopped cilantro

COMBINE water, salsa, seasoning mix and oil in large saucepan; mix well. Stir in rice and beans; mix well.

BRING to a boil over medium-high heat. Cover; remove from heat. Let stand 5 minutes.

STIR in cilantro. *Makes 4 servings*

Country-Style Corn

4 strips bacon
1 tablespoon flour
1 tablespoon sugar
2 cans (about 15 ounces each) cream-style corn
Salt and black pepper

1. Cook bacon in large skillet over medium heat until crisp; drain on paper towel. Crumble bacon; set aside.

2. Whisk flour and sugar into drippings. Add corn to skillet. Bring to a boil. Reduce heat to low. Cook 15 minutes or until liquid thickens.

3. Stir bacon into corn. Season with salt and pepper.

Makes 6 to 8 servings

Acorn Squash with Corn Bread Stuffing

1 acorn squash (about 2 pounds)
¼ cup (½ stick) butter, divided
2 cups chopped mushrooms
1 medium onion, chopped
1 stalk celery, chopped
¾ cup seasoned corn bread stuffing mix
¼ teaspoon salt
¼ teaspoon black pepper
2 tablespoons packed brown sugar, divided

1. Preheat oven to 375°F. Cut squash into quarters; remove and discard seeds. Place squash, skin side up, in microwavable dish; add ½ inch water. Cover loosely with plastic wrap; microwave on HIGH 8 to 10 minutes or until tender.* Drain well.

2. Meanwhile, melt 2 tablespoons butter in large saucepan over medium heat. Add mushrooms, onion and celery; cook and stir 7 to 10 minutes or until tender. Remove from heat. Stir in stuffing mix, salt and pepper.

3. Place squash in baking dish, cut-side up. Top each quarter with 1½ teaspoons butter and 1½ teaspoons brown sugar. Pack ½ cup stuffing onto each quarter. Bake 25 to 30 minutes or until stuffing is golden brown. *Makes 4 servings*

To cook on stovetop, place squash quarters in large saucepan with boiling water to cover. Cook 30 minutes or until fork tender. Drain well.

Potluck Tip: To bring Acorn Squash with Corn Bread Stuffing as a potluck dish, prepare the squash as directed in step 1; cover and refrigerate up to one day. Prepare the stuffing as directed in step 2; cover and refrigerate up to one day. To serve, assemble the squash at your host's home as directed in step 3; bake at 375°F for 25 to 30 minutes. Or wrap the baked dish in several layers of foil and wrap again with a thick towel or newspapers to keep the finished dish warm while transporting.

Stovetop Summer Squash

1⅔ **cups water**
1 **package (6 ounces) stuffing mix with herb**
   seasoning packet
3 **tablespoons butter**
1 **cup chopped onion**
1 **cup chopped red bell pepper**
1 **tablespoon minced fresh basil**
2 **cups sliced yellow squash**
2 **cups sliced zucchini**

1. Bring water to a boil in 2-quart saucepan. Add seasoning packet from stuffing mix; cover and cook over low heat 15 minutes.

2. Meanwhile, melt butter in large skillet over medium heat. Add onion and bell pepper; cook and stir 3 minutes or until tender. Add basil, squash and zucchini; cook and stir about 3 minutes or until vegetables are tender.

3. Add squash mixture and stuffing mix to hot water; Stir until all liquid is absorbed. Remove from heat; cover and let stand 5 minutes. Fluff with fork before serving.   *Makes 6 servings*

Green Beans and Red Onion with Mustard Vinaigrette

1½ pounds fresh green beans, trimmed
1 cup sliced red onion
3 tablespoons red wine vinegar
2 tablespoons Dijon mustard
1 tablespoon olive oil
¼ teaspoon salt
¼ teaspoon black pepper

1. Cook green beans in boiling water 8 minutes or until crisp-tender. Drain beans. Combine green beans and onion in large bowl.

2. Whisk vinegar, mustard, olive oil, salt and pepper together in microwavable bowl. Cook mixture on HIGH 1 minute. Remove from microwave and whisk mixture.

3. Drizzle dressing over bean mixture. Toss well to coat.
Makes 6 servings (1 cup per serving)

Honey and Vanilla Glazed Carrots

¼ cup (½ stick) butter or margarine
¼ cup honey
1½ pounds baby carrots (about 5 cups), cooked
**   until crisp-tender**
1½ teaspoons WATKINS® Vanilla Extract
**   Pinch WATKINS® Ginger**
**   Salt and WATKINS® Black Pepper to taste**

Melt butter in medium saucepan. Add honey and stir until blended. Add carrots, vanilla and ginger. Cook over low heat, stirring occasionally, until carrots are well glazed. Season with salt and pepper.
Makes 10 servings (5 cups)

Spicy Skillet Vegetables, Salsa-Style

2 cups finely diced peeled potatoes
½ cup water
2 tablespoons vegetable oil
1 green bell pepper, cut into strips
1 red bell pepper, cut into strips
1 jar (16 ounces) ORTEGA® Salsa, any variety
1 can (about 15 ounces) black beans, rinsed and drained
1 can (15 ounces) corn, drained
⅓ cup ORTEGA Diced Jalapeños
1 cup (4 ounces) crumbled queso fresco or shredded Monterey Jack cheese

MICROWAVE potatoes with water, covered, on HIGH (100%) 5 minutes. Drain. In large skillet, heat oil over medium-high heat.

COOK and stir bell pepper strips in skillet for 3 to 4 minutes. Stir in drained potatoes and salsa, then beans, corn and jalapeños.

BRING to a boil. Cover; reduce heat to medium and cook for 5 minutes, or until potatoes are tender.

SPRINKLE with cheese before serving.

Makes 8 servings (1 cup each)

*Tip

If jalapeños are too hot for your family, use diced green chiles instead.

Fiesta-Style Roasted Vegetables

1 can (4 ounces) ORTEGA® Diced Green Chiles
3 tablespoons vinegar
2 tablespoons vegetable oil
1 package (1.25 ounces) ORTEGA Taco Seasoning Mix
1 small red bell pepper, cut into strips
1 medium zucchini, cut into ½-inch slices
1 small sweet potato, peeled, halved and cut into ⅛-inch slices
1 small red onion, cut into wedges
Nonstick cooking spray

COMBINE chiles, vinegar, oil and seasoning mix in large bowl; mix well. Add red pepper, zucchini, sweet potato and onion; toss gently to coat. Let stand at room temperature 15 minutes to marinate.

PREHEAT oven to 450°F. Cover 15×10-inch baking pan with foil and spray with cooking spray.

REMOVE vegetables from marinade with spoon; place on prepared pan.

BAKE 20 to 25 minutes until tender and browned, stirring once.

Makes 4 servings

*Tip

Substitute yellow squash for the zucchini, if preferred.

Lemon Icebox Pie
(p. 90)

Cheesecake Cookie Bars
(p. 88)

White Chocolate Macadamia
Cupcakes (p. 86)

Tortoise Snack Cake
(p. 92)

Super Sweets

White Chocolate Macadamia Cupcakes

1 package (18¼ ounces) white cake mix, plus
    ingredients to prepare mix
1 package (4-serving size) white chocolate instant
    pudding and pie filling mix
¾ cup chopped macadamia nuts
1½ cups flaked coconut
1 cup white chocolate chips
1 container (16 ounces) white frosting

1. Preheat oven to 350°F. Line 20 standard (2½-inch) muffin cups with paper baking cups.

2. Prepare cake mix according to package directions, beating in pudding mix with cake mix ingredients. Fold in nuts. Fill prepared muffin cups two-thirds full.

3. Bake 18 to 20 minutes or until toothpick inserted into centers comes out clean. Cool cupcakes in pans on wire racks 10 minutes. Remove to racks; cool completely.

4. Meanwhile, spread coconut evenly on ungreased baking sheet; bake at 350°F 6 minutes or until light golden brown, stirring occasionally. Cool completely.

5. Place white chocolate chips in small microwavable bowl; microwave 2 minutes on MEDIUM (50%), stirring every 30 seconds, until melted and smooth. Cool slightly before stirring into frosting. Frost cupcakes; sprinkle with toasted coconut.

Makes 20 cupcakes

Cheesecake Cookie Bars

2 packages (18 ounces each) refrigerated chocolate chip cookie dough
2 packages (8 ounces each) cream cheese, softened
½ cup sugar
2 eggs

1. Preheat oven to 350°F. Lightly grease 13×9-inch baking pan. Let both packages of dough stand at room temperature about 15 minutes.

2. Reserve three-fourths of one package of dough. Press remaining 1¼ packages of dough evenly onto bottom of prepared pan.

3. Combine cream cheese, sugar and eggs in large bowl; beat until well blended and smooth. Spread cream cheese mixture over dough in pan. Break reserved dough into small pieces; sprinkle over cream cheese mixture.

4. Bake 35 minutes or until center is almost set. Cool completely in pan on wire rack. Store leftovers covered in refrigerator.

Makes about 2 dozen bars

Chocolate Peanut Butter Pie

1 can (14 ounces) sweetened condensed milk
¼ cup creamy peanut butter
2 tablespoons unsweetened cocoa powder
1 container (8 ounces) thawed whipped topping
1 (6-ounce) chocolate cookie crumb crust

1. Beat condensed milk, peanut butter and cocoa in large bowl with electric mixer at medium speed until smooth and well blended. Fold in whipped topping. Pour mixture into crust.

2. Freeze at least 6 hours or overnight.

Makes 6 to 8 servings

Lemon
Icebox Pie

**1 (14-ounce) can EAGLE BRAND® Sweetened
Condensed Milk (NOT evaporated milk)**
½ cup lemon juice
   Yellow food coloring (optional)
1 cup (½ pint) whipping cream, whipped
**1 (6-ounce) prepared graham cracker or baked pie
crust**

1. In medium bowl, combine EAGLE BRAND®, lemon juice and food coloring (optional). Fold in whipped cream. Pour into crust.

2. Chill 3 hours or until set. Garnish as desired. Store leftovers covered in refrigerator.   *Makes one (6-ounce) pie*

White Chocolate
Pudding Parfaits

2 cups milk
**1 package (4-serving size) white chocolate instant
pudding and pie filling mix**
¾ cup cold whipping cream
1½ cups fresh raspberries or sliced strawberries
**2 tablespoons chopped shelled pistachio nuts or
chopped toasted macadamia nuts**

1. Combine milk and pudding mix in medium bowl; beat 2 minutes. Refrigerate 5 minutes or until thickened. Beat whipping cream in clean bowl with electric mixer at high speed until stiff peaks form. Fold whipped cream into pudding.

2. Layer ¼ cup pudding and 2 tablespoons raspberries in each of 4 parfait glasses; repeat layers. Spoon remaining pudding over berries. Serve immediately or cover and refrigerate up to 6 hours before serving. Sprinkle with nuts just before serving.
Makes 4 servings

Tortoise Snack Cake

1 package (about 18 ounces) devil's food cake mix,
plus ingredients to prepare mix
1 cup chopped pecans
1 cup semisweet chocolate chips
½ teaspoon vanilla
½ cup caramel sauce
Additional caramel sauce and chopped pecans

1. Preheat oven to 350°F. Grease 13×9-inch baking pan.

2. Prepare cake mix according to package directions. Stir pecans, chocolate chips and vanilla into batter. Pour into prepared pan. Drizzle ½ cup caramel sauce over batter; swirl caramel into batter with knife.

3. Bake 32 minutes or until cake begins to pull away from sides of pan and toothpick inserted into center comes out clean. Cool slightly on wire rack. Top each serving with additional caramel sauce and pecans.   *Makes 24 servings*

*Tip

Keep pecans on hand for a variety of snacks and desserts. They can be stored in an airtight container up to 3 months in the refrigerator and up to 6 months in the freezer.

The publisher would like to thank the companies and organizations listed below for the use of their recipes and photographs in this publication.

Bays English Muffin Corporation

Birds Eye Foods

Bob Evans®

CanolaInfo

Del Monte Corporation

Dole Food Company, Inc.

EAGLE BRAND®

Guiltless Gourmet®

Heinz North America

Hormel Foods, LLC

National Pork Board

Ortega®, A Division of B&G Foods, Inc.

Reckitt Benckiser Inc.

Unilever

Veg•All®

Watkins Incorporated

Wisconsin Milk Marketing Board